The Strife of Brian

ANDY DONATO

The Strife of Brian

Political Cartoons

KEY PORTER·BOOKS

A collection of cartoons that appeared in *The Toronto Sun*

Key Porter Books Limited
70 The Esplanade
Toronto, Ontario
M5E 1R2

Design: *First Image*
Printing and binding: *Webcom*

Printed and bound in Canada

87 88 89 4 3 2 1

Introduction

by Christie Blatchford

There's a mean old line about the people who write editorials at newspapers — that they're the guys who come down from the hill, *after* the battle is over, to shoot the wounded.

It's not a bad description of the breed (or the job, for that matter), and it may also fit some of the men and women who draw the cartoons that illustrate those ivory-tower pronouncements, but it sure isn't Andy Donato.

Donato is a front-line kind of cartoonist, the sort who doesn't mind getting his hands a little dirty, which is why the *Sun* regularly sends him to such diverse events as political conventions (where he produces, on demand and on time, entire *pages* of wicked stuff) and major-league baseball's spring training camps in Florida (where he comes up with centrespreads in full-color now known as "Donato-vision").

All this, mind you, Donato does in addition to his daily cartoons for the *Sun*, his job as art director for the paper (which means that, against all the time-worn traditions of journalists, he can even manage a budget and staff), a sideline as creative director of *Influence* (the magazine, run by former *Sun* editor Peter Worthington) and, of course, his art (which is, unlike Donato, both realist and serious). The amazing part is that most days he also manages to squeeze in 18 holes of golf.

That he rarely *seems* busy is part of his charm; that in person, he's every bit as kind as he is biting and satirical in print is the miracle, and the pleasure.

Men describe him, readily and a little gleefully, as a man's man. It's easy to see why — he's a comfortable sort of fellow, a bit of a joker, and until recently, was a viciously competitive catcher (which is why one of his fingers is a little bent) who had the ability, says one of his former teammates, "to appear to be going about 100 miles an hour around the bases when really, he was dogging it at five mph."

Women like him just as much: My spies in the *Sun*'s secretarial ranks, who see Donato every year at the paper's wing-ding lunch on Secretary's Day, say he's an accomplished, enjoyable flirt — which, when you think about it, is by and large a lost art these days.

I like him for that reason too, but mostly because he's the only man I know who, like *every* woman I know, has separate wardrobes to match his separate shapes, which vary according to the time of year. "This is my summer body," he says, when looking particularly trim. "The winter one's a heluva lot bigger."

Given that he's won a National Newspaper Award for cartooning and first prize in the prestigious International Salon of Cartoons and been named president of the Association of American Editorial Cartoonists (they even have conventions, which is an unnerving thought), the wonder is that he's able to keep the size of his ego under control.

It's one mark of the real professional, and Donato is definitely that, and more of an all-round newspaper-man than most reporters. And you know what else? He makes me wish *I* could draw — that round-cheeked, mobile face, framed by fuzz . . . Andy Donato, the journalist's cartoonist, is also a cartoonist's dream.

AN IMPORTANT MESSAGE FROM CANADA POST

To insure prompt delivery of your mail be sure to post all letters in postal boxes situated in elevated areas.

DONATO *TORONTO SUN*

Canada
Post

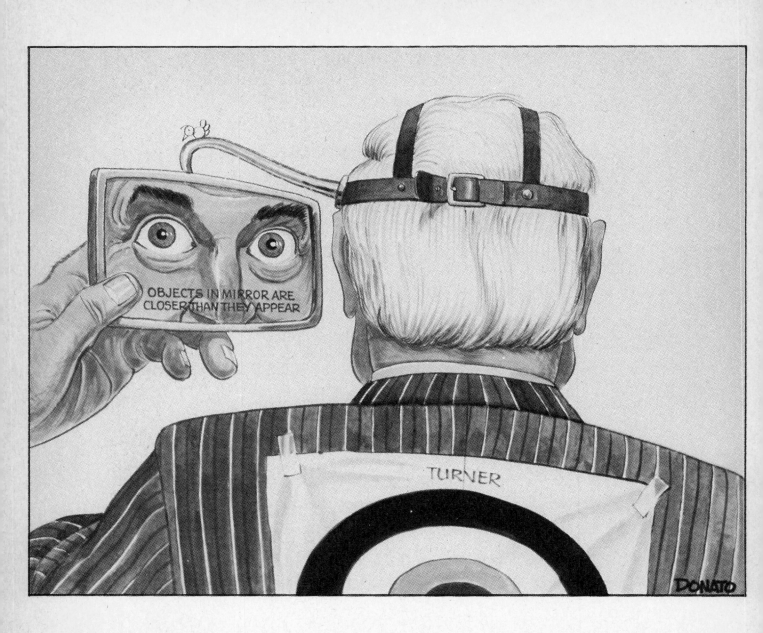

THE IRON LADY

LAME DUCK

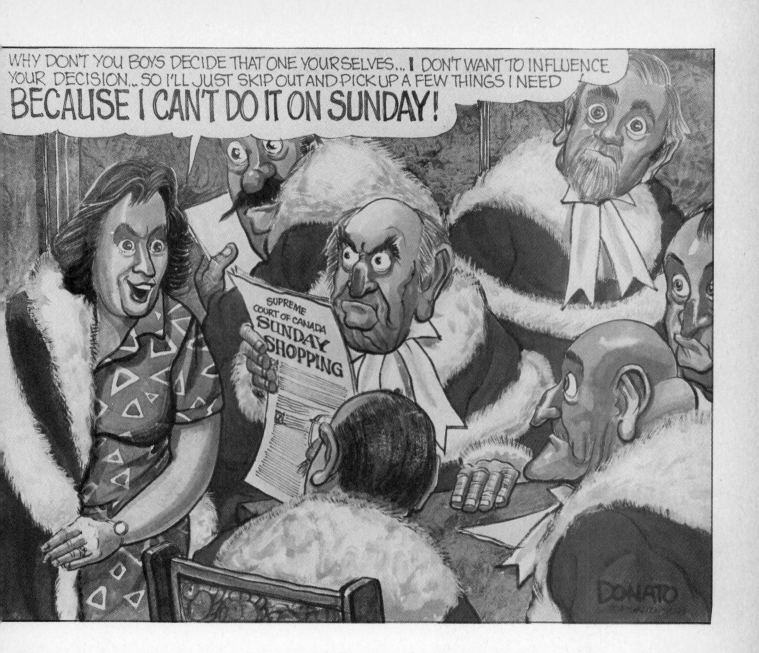

PRESENTED TO THE
SOVIET EMBASSY
ON BEHALF OF
THE CITIZENS OF
THE UNITED STATES

DONATO
TORONTO SUN

MR. BAZIN IS IN FACT A CLOSE PERSONAL FRIEND!

HE HAS SERVED HIS COUNTRY WELL...

...AND WORKED HARD, NOT ONLY FOR THE PARTY, BUT FOR ALL OF CANADA!

THIS IS A MAN WHO KNOWS INDUSTRY...

OERLIKON THOUGHT SO MUCH OF HIS WORK THEY MADE HIM A DIRECTOR!

THIS GOVERNMENT THOUGHT SO MUCH OF HIS DEDICATION I MADE HIM A SENATOR!

HE KNOWS THE PARTY..., HE KNOWS INDUSTRY... HE KNOWS GOVERNMENT

BUT MORE THAN THAT...

HE KNOWS REAL ESTATE!

DONATO TORONTO STAR

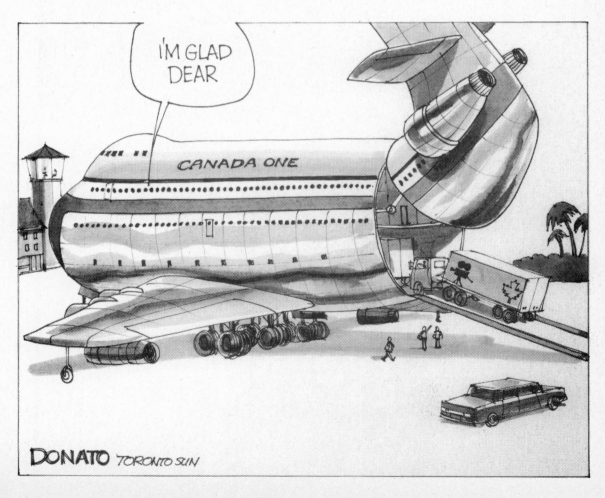

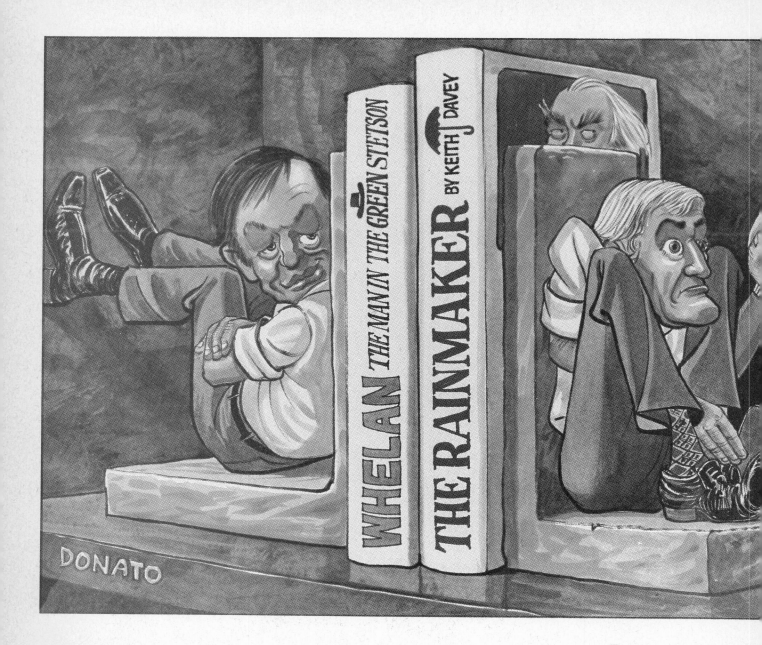

Maclean's
THE RAINMAKER
DAVEY BREAKS OUT

DONATO
TORONTO SUN

Donato's Believe It or Not!

QUEEN'S PARK, TORONTO, CANADA
WHEN HEADS ROLL IN ONTARIO'S CAPITAL
NOT ONLY DO THE BODIES STAY ATTACHED BUT
THEY GATHER MONEY AS THEY ROLL!

DONATO
TORONTO SUN

DONATO *TORONTO SUN*

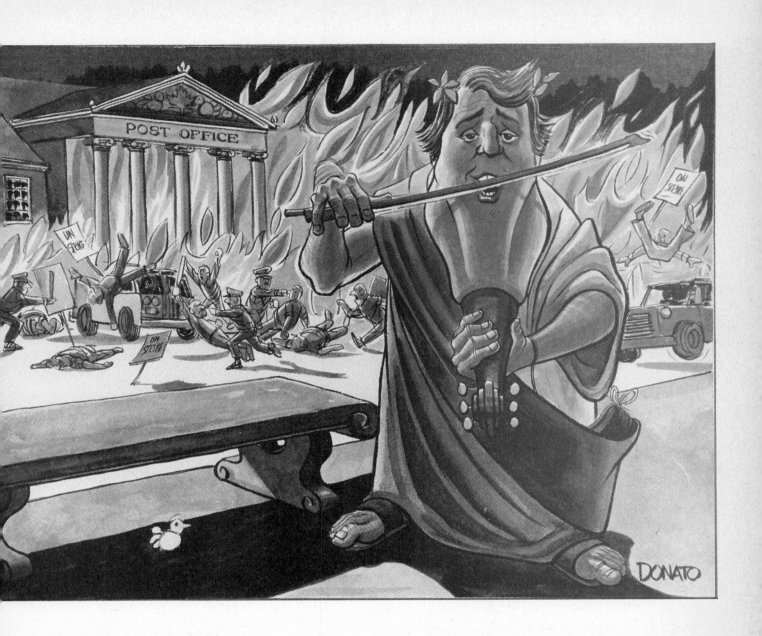

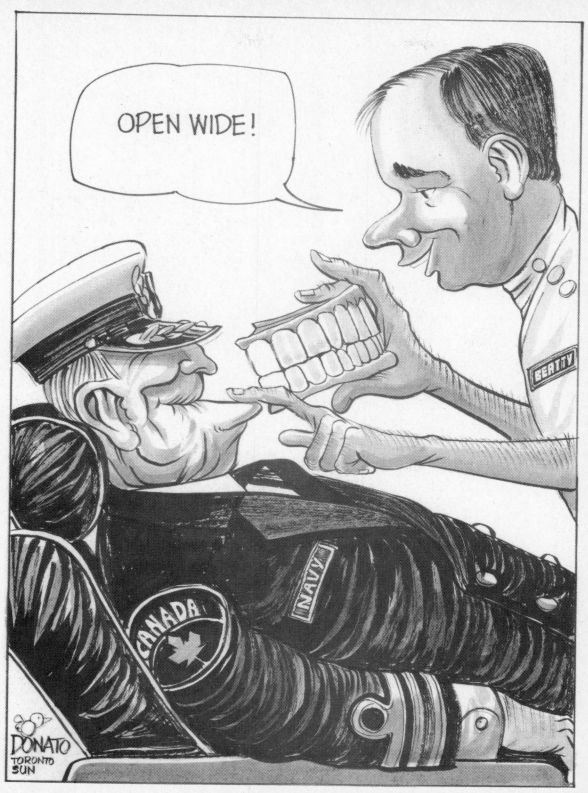

TEETH, AT LAST

DONATO TORONTO SUN

DONATO *TORONTO SUN*

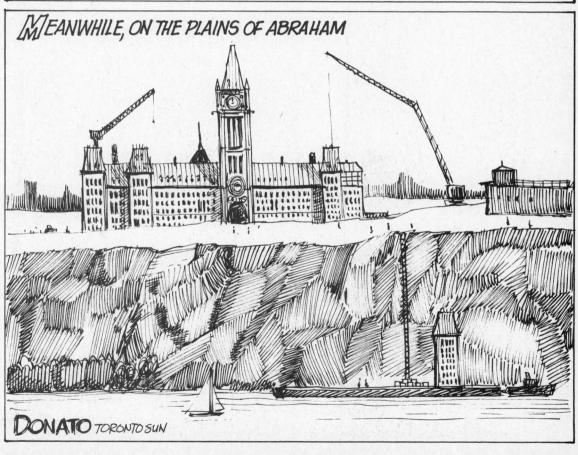

MIKE

1987
BUDGET
SHOES

DONATO *TORONTO SUN*

DONATO *TORONTO SUN*

DONATO *TORONTO SUN*

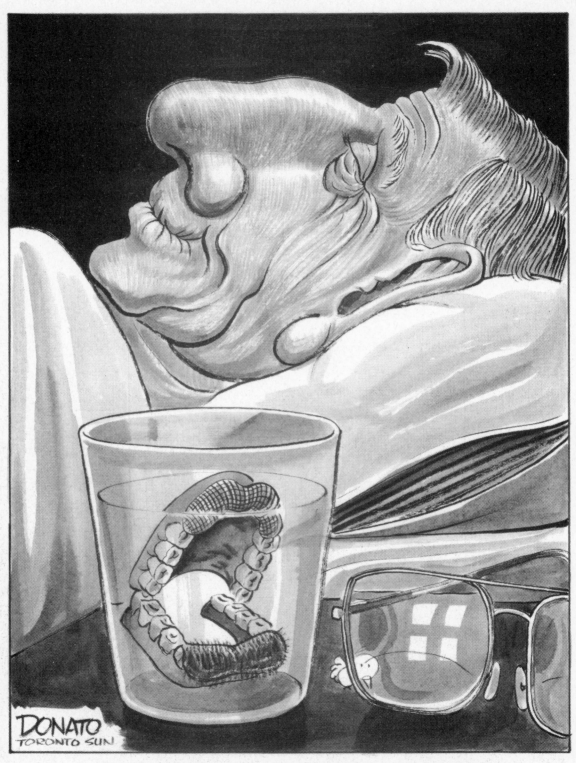

OLD VELCRO LIPS HAS FINALLY RETIRED

TO MY PAL
BRIAN
LOVE
RON!

DONATO
TORONTO SUN

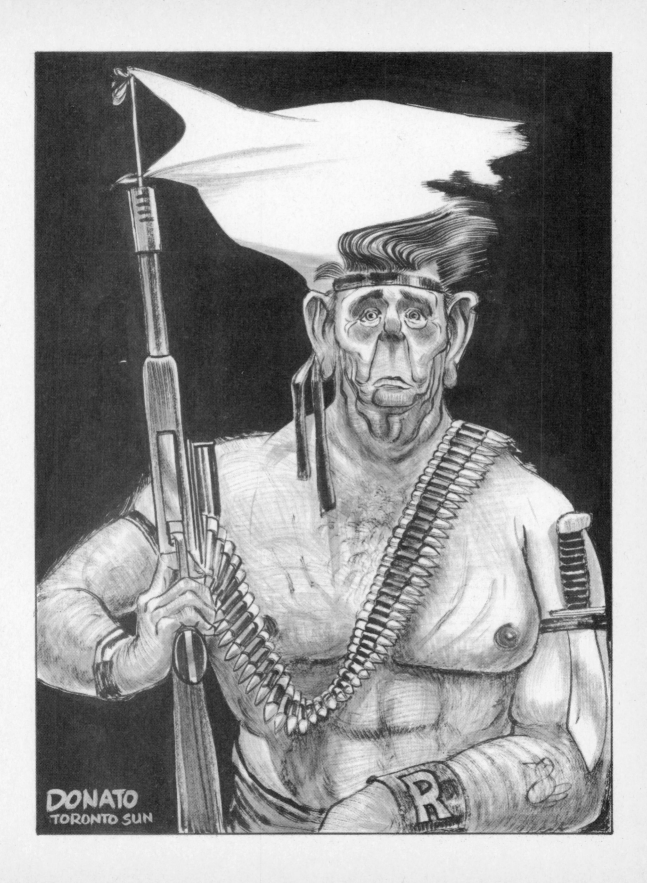

DONATO
TORONTO SUN

MULDOON COUNTRY

WITH APOLOGIES TO **BERKE BREATHED**

TWO HOURS AND THE COWBOY ARRIVES

WELL THIS TIME, IRISH EYES WON'T BE SMILING! THIS TIME IT'S THE COLD STARE... NO BLINKING! I'M GOING TO BE TOUGH AS STEEL, HARD AS NAILS!

CLICK

I'LL JUST SUCK UP AN HOUR OF BRONSON, STALLONE AND EASTWOOD OFF THE TUBE AND GET PUMPED UP TO MEET BONZO!

GEEZ THAT WAS GREAT, NOW I'M READY FOR THAT YANKEE TRADIN', ACID MAKIN' ARCTIC TRESPASSER!

THIS IS GOIN' TO BE GOOD!

SOMEHOW I DON'T THINK THIS IS GOING TO LOOK TOO GOOD ON THE ELEVEN O'CLOCK NEWS

DONATO

DONATO TORONTO SUN

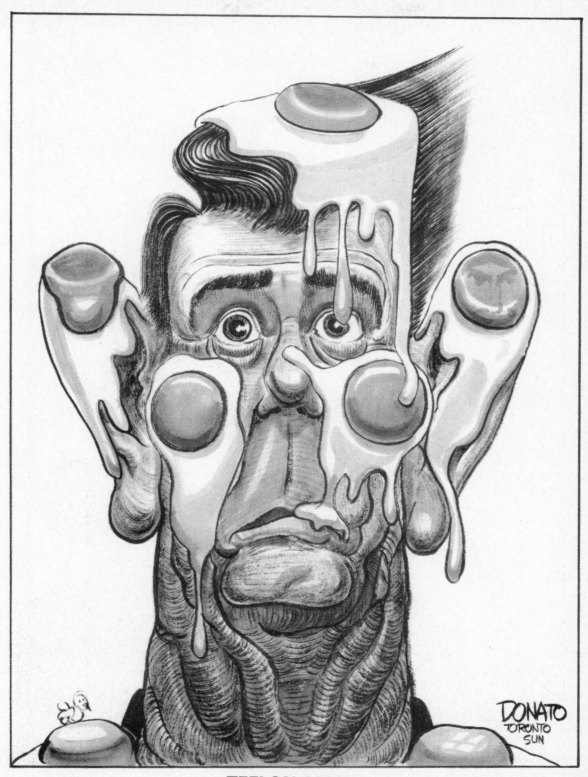

TEFLON MAN

WELL RENE... I'M GLAD YOU'RE BACK... YOU WON THE BYELECTION AND THAT'S GREAT... BUT YOU KNOW, WITH ALL THIS STUFF ABOUT YOUR 'LUMBER INTERESTS'...

WELL...AS MUCH AS I'D LIKE YOU TO BE BACK IN THE CABINET... I THINK IT WOULD BE BETTER IF YOU SAT, FOR THE TIME BEING, AS A BACK BENCHER!

BE PATIENT!

DONATO TORONTO SUN

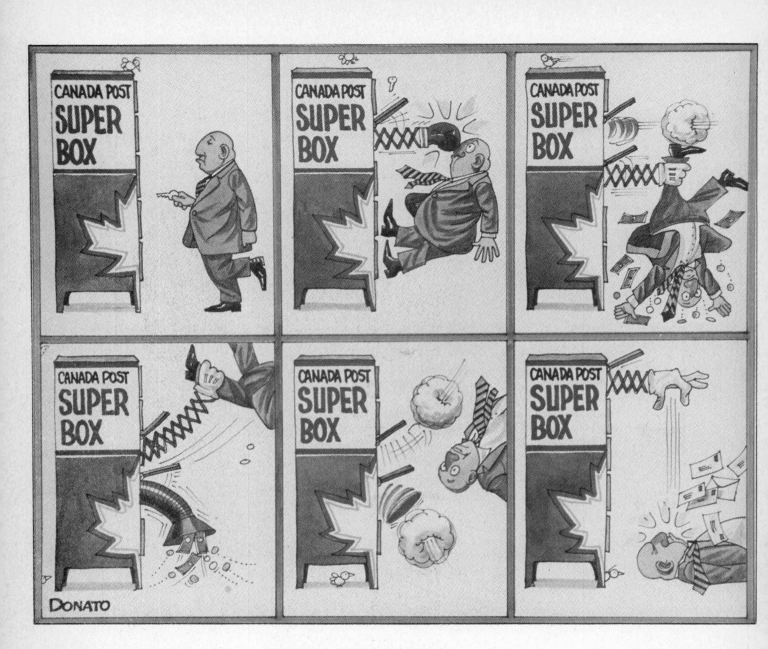

MULDOON COUNTRY WITH APOLOGIES TO BERKE BREATHED

THE EASTER BREAK IS OVER... NOW IT'S BACK TO THE REAL WORLD

I HATE FACING THOSE ANIMALS IN QUESTION PERIOD!

GAD! THERE ARE SEVENTY MEMBERS OF THE OPPOSITION! SEVENTY!

DONATO TORONTO SUN

I'VE GOT ALMOST THAT MANY PAIRS OF SHOES IN MY CLOSET!